CRICUT EXPLORE 3 MADE EASY

BEGINNERS GUIDE ON HOW TO USE THE CRICUT MACHINE FOR DIY PROJECTS

Rose Macar

TABLE OF CONTENTS

Chapter One

Introduction

Cricut Explore 3 machine are sleek and versatile cutting machines. It is a crafting machine that is used in cutting and drawing on a wide range of materials. This machine can used for graphic design on a wall. It can be used to write and cut a welcome sign on a house. It cuts twice as fast as the old model. It can also cut over 100 different materials. With the use of an app (Design space) on your phone, computer, tablet etc you can gain access projects, shapes, fonts, decorations, images and more instead of buying cartridges.

The Cricut Explore 3 cutting machine is perfect for beginner hobbyists. The Explore 3 machine can cut over 100 different materials. It can also cut large scale projects up to 12 foot long when using Smart Materials. With the ability to cut lengthy projects, it can cut without the use of a mat. Cricut explore 3 is less technical than cricut maker 3.

What is Cricut Explore 3

See your creativity skyrocket with this latest release from Cricut Explore family called Cricut Explore 3. Cricut Explore 3 is an electronic device that can cut more than 100 materials ranging from vinyl and iron-on, cardstock, to glitter paper and bonded fabric. It works perfectly well with Cricut Smart Materials which you have to purchase from the store, for easy and long cut up to 3.6m without the need for a separate cutting mat. It is highly versatile. It can be used with design space spp for windows, Mac, Andriod, and iOS, it also has a slot for phones and a built-in storage cubby for added convenience. It has a Fine-Point Blade and it is designed to work with the scoring stylus and Deep-Point Blade for handling a variety of craft materials. It works with Cricut Foil transfer Tool which you also need to buy from the store, this Foil transfer tool adds pro-level embellishments to your creativity. Cricut Explore 3 allows you to cut, draw, score, and do a variety of other tasks with breakneck speed and precision. Smart Materials are compatible with the Cricut Explore 3 for super-easy, super-long cuts up to 12 ft (3.6 m) without a mat – simply load and go! It's also up to twice as quick as its predecessor, allowing you to produce everything from bespoke iron-ons to large banners in record time. Cricut Explore 3 comes with six distinct tools for cutting and decorating 100+ materials like cardstock, vinyl, iron-on, glitter paper, cork, and bonded fabric, with this you can draw, cut, write, score, foil etc. In fact, with Cricut Explore 3 your crafting possibilities are endless. Ideal for small-scale craft projects or large-scale DIY projects. Use in conjunction with the Design Space® app for iOS®, AndroidTM, Windows®, and Mac®.

Content of Cricut Explore 3

1x Cricut Explore 3 itself

1x Material for practice cuts

1x Adaptive tool housing

1x USB cable

1x welcome card (Quick start card, warranty paper and safety paper)

1x premium Fine Point Blade and blade housing (pre-installed in clamp B)
1x Accessory adapter (pre-installed in clamp A)

1x 100 ready-to-make projects online

1x power cord and power adapter
1x Free trial subscription to Cricut Access™ (for new subscribers)
A park of bonus materials

Chapter Two

How Cricut Explore 3 is Designed

The machine has enough compact that enables it sit on the desk close to a computer, tablet, etc. it has a small holder that can hold a phone while the device is in operation. Once you push a button the door snaps open and locks with ease and securely when you're done with crafting. It comes with a USB cable that connects it to a computer or tablet, you can also use Bluetooth to connect it to an android device, iPhone, iPad. It works perfectly well with PC devices and Mac. It is very easy to set up, within few minutes of unboxing, you can get to connected to your device and boom! you can start crafting. If you decide to work with Smart material for long cuts, there is a handy material holder that help keep your Smart Material on a roll for easy feeding and cutting. From power cord plugs into the back. To open the machine lift the lid and you will notice the door opens automatically.

Be sure to remove the protective foam place on it. The first thing you will notice in Explore 3 is that it does not have material dial. Cricut went for a sleeker design that can cut different materials.

So with Cricut Explore 3 you can select your material from Design Space and not from dial. You will also notice that the bottom of the machine is smooth while the top features are textured coating. The purpose of this is to keep it from collecting fingerprints and its implication is that time is conserved, and you become more productive (More time for crafting instead of cleaning your machine). The name is also boldly written on the housing tool, that means you remember the name of the machine you are using by just looking at it. You will also notice that it has updated its color. Isn't that lovely? It is! The mint color of Explore 3 is more intense than its predecessor. It also has an expanded storage cup. That means you can store more tools and blades in this storage cup. It also has a more advanced light sensor which allows you print and cut your projects using colored paper. The "C" button that's on older models has been replaced with a more universal start button. It has a docking slot on the lid where you can keep your device especially if you're working with phone. When you purchase Cricut Explore 3, it comes with a sample of each of their Smart Materials so that you can see it and appreciate its beauty.

Chapter Three

How to set up your Cricut Explore 3 (step by step)

1. After unboxing, plug in your machine to a power source and power it on
2. Connect your cricut explore 3 to your device either computer, or laptop, or android device using USB cord or you can connect it via Bluetooth pairing. Follow this step to pair your device with your machine via Bluetooth; with your machine already powered on, ensure it is within 12-15 feet of your computer(device). Most computers are Bluetooth enabled but if yours does not have you can buy USB device known as Bluetooth Dongle. To check if your device has Bluetooth right click on the start button and select **device**

Manager, if Bluetooth is listed, it then means that your device is Bluetooth enabled. Close the device manager, open the start menu and select settings, click on devices to open it, ensure that the Bluetooth is on, then click on add Bluetooth or other device(s). Select Bluetooth and wait until your computer detects your Cricut Explore 3. Select the machine from the list. If PIN is requested type 0000 and select connect. And yes! Your cricut explore 3 has been paired with your computer(device).

3. Then log on to design.cricut.com/setup explore 3 in your browser to get Design space
4. Download and install your Design Space

5. Follow the promptings on your screen to sign in to create your Cricut ID and password and set up your machine
6. If you are instructed to test a cut, it then means that your setup is complete and ready to run

Getting started with Design Space

Design space is a free software used with Cricut smart cutting machine such as Cricut Maker 3, Cricut Explore 3. Design space is not compatible on Linux/Unixcomputers and chromebook. If you already have a background knowledge of photoshop, design space will be very easy and simple for you to navigate through but in a situation where you are a beginner, let me take you through step by step approach to using Design Space, ready? Let's go!

Design space can run on Andriod, Windows, Mac computer or on your iOS. To download this software you have to go to design.cricut.com/setup explore 3 no your browser. Select download. When the download is complete, double-click or right click the file in your download folder or browser. A window will open to ask if you trust the trust the application, select yes. After this a setup window will display the installation progress. Sign in with your cricut explore 3 ID and password. The design space will automatically be added to your desktop. Note that this software does not auto-save your work, ensure you save it as often as possible and before you logout. If after using the app you logged out, you will have to sign in when next you want to make use of the design space.

Chapter Four

What Cricut Explore 3 can do

It can cut

It can write

It can draw

It can also score

It can foil with over 100 different materials that are compactible

Cricut Explore 3 can work with the following:

- Scoring stylus
- Bonded fabric blade
- Foil transfer system
- Fine-point blade
- Deep-point blade

The amazing thing with Smart Materials is that it saves time, it also allow you cut 2X faster than the Cricut Explore previous model. With smart materials your machine can cut up to 8 inches per second on each axis. You can cut up to 12 feet at a go and this makes it perfect for large wall decals and group t-shirts. This machine needs at least 6 inches in length to load into the machine but if you purchased scrap Smart Materials that are smaller than this, you can place it on Mat to enable you use them. Cricut Explore 3 has three different Smart Materials and they are; smart paper sticker cardstock, smart vinyl and smart iron-on

- Smart Paper Sticker Cardstock: it has a double-sided adhesive that lets you skip the glue for a project that is not messy, you just need to peel and stick. It enables you to load a sheet in the machine without a Mat. You can purchase variety packs with a single color or multiple color each pack comes with 10sheets with each measuring 13" by 13" and you can cut 11.7" by 11.2". You can use to cut any kind of paper project ranging from card-paper, birthday banner.

- Smart Vinyl: it comes in different colors, effects and material lengths (3ft -75ft) in both permanent and removable adhesives. With it is needless to place vinyl up on a mat, you just have to load your machine and start crafting.

- Smart Iron-On : its available in glitter, solid and holographic varieties. It comes in variety of colors and length and it is just so perfect for large project. It can cut image up to 4ft. with it you can make custom T-shirt

Cricut Machine Tools and Blades

Cricut Machine Tools

Foil Transfer Tool

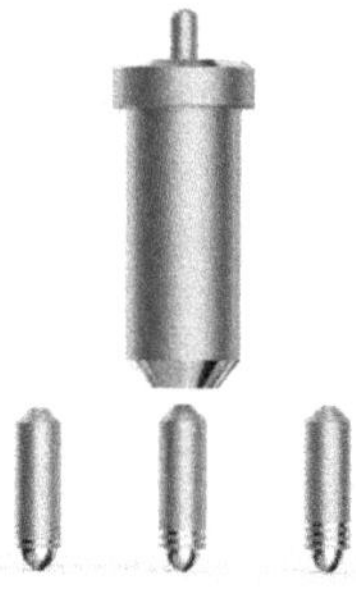

The Foil Transfer Tool is used with Foil Transfer Sheets to add a foil effect to projects on a variety of materials. It comes with 3 interchangeable tips – fine, medium, and bold – all suitable for projects ranging from simple outlines to intricate designs. Also compatible with Cricut Maker machines.

Scoring Stylus

The Scoring Stylus: it allows you use your Cricut Explore machine to score fold lines for cards and envelopes, 3D projects, boxes, and more. Cricut Explore holds the Scoring Stylus and a cutting blade at the same time, enabling you to cut and score in one step, changing mats is not needed! It also works with Cricut Maker.

Roll Holder

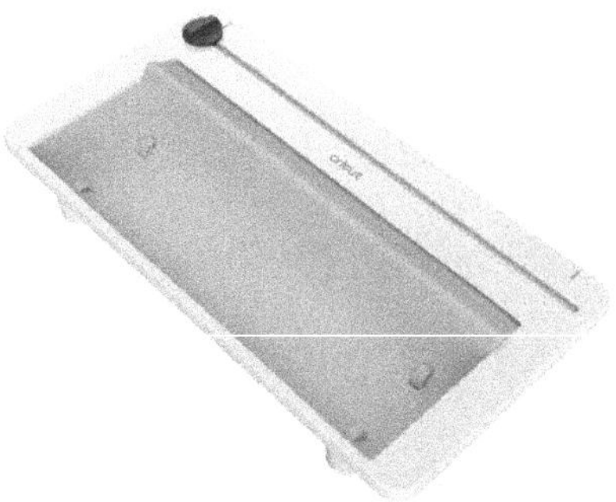

Cricut Roll Holder works with Cricut Explore 3 and Cricut Maker 3 to manage rolls of Smart Materials and keep them perfectly aligned during cutting. Cricut Explore 3 Fine-Point Blades are colour coded, you get to know which blade to use on a material by mere looking at the blade

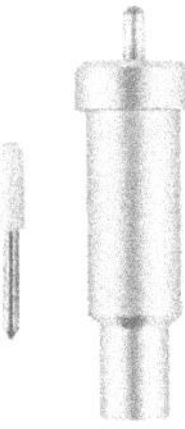

Premium Fine-Point Blade

Premium Fine-Point blade is designed to make the most difficult cuts possible in a variety of thin to medium-weight materials. It was formerly called Premium German Carbide blade because it is made from premium German carbide steel.

- It is used alongside silver Fine-Point Housing or gold Premium Fine-Point Housing
- Recommended for use with poster board, paper, iron-on, cardstock, vinyl, and any other thin to medium weight materials
- Premium Fine-Point blade and housing are compatible with all Cricut Maker and Cricut Explore machines
- Premium Fine-Point blades are gold in color and very beautiful.

Deep Point Blade

Deep-point blade makes it easy to perform complex cuts on an extensive variety of materials for your projects. The Deep point blade has a steeper blade angle (60 degrees vs 45 degrees for the other fine point blades) and harder, more durable steel. It is one of Fine

- Recommended for intricate cuts on thicker materials, such as magnet, chipboard, stamp material, thick cardstock, stiffened felt, foam sheets, cardboard, and some fabrics

- Deep-Point blades are black in color and fine too
- It must be used with the Deep-Point Blade Housing
- This blade and housing can be used with all Cricut Maker and Cricut Explore machines

How much is Cricut Explore 3 and where can I buy it?

Cricut Explore 3 was made available online in June 10, 2021 and in stores in June 27th, so you can either decide to get it online at cricut.com or from online retailers or from stores. The current price of Cricut explore 3 is $299. Cricut Explore 3 accessories can also be purchased online

Cricut Explore 3 Accessories

Because of Smart Materials Cricut upgraded their portable trimmer. The portable trimmer became a little bit bigger to accommodate

Smart materials that are now 13" wide. The built-in trimmer ensures a straight edge at eth end of your project. As you cut your projects, the roll holder holds your projects neatly rolled up. When you're done cutting, the machine positions the end of your cut above the trimmer. Before you unload your project, just slide the trimmer across for a neat, straight cut. To ensure that materials does not roll off your table especially if you're working with projects, just get Smart Material Rolls, it can hold up to a 75-foot roll and its easier. If you're making more vinyl and Iron-On projects, then the Roll Holder is a must have for you. It is compatible with Cricut Explore 3 and Maker 3 only. It attaches to the tray of the machine to hold rolled materials aligned for easy, clean and precise cuts.

How to measure material for your cut

Cricut Explore 3 has a sensor and this sensor measure your material length for you. So before you start cutting, your machine will measure your material for you, it will also notify you if your material is not enough, you simply have to load a piece of Smart Material into your machine that is enough to continue your cut and you're good to go!

Projects that can done using Cricut Explore 3

Creativity lies inside everyone, with Cricut Explore 3 your remarkable story can be designed and shared through imaginative work always.

Iron-On: With material having variety of effects, colors etc Iron-On materials are perfect for customizing T-shirt, bags, pillows, scarves birthday cards and many more. Just cut a design and then use Iron-On to apply it to your craft. Create customized printed stickers, iron-on, decals in minutes. Use your printer to print designs on your chosen material, then use the Print then cut feature in Design Space to flawlessly cut around them. Print on sticker paper, iron-on, magnetic sheet and vinyl.

Paper crafts for parties and every occasion

Use original Cricut material of your choice to craft. Smart Paper Sticker Cardstock comes in different colors, weight, finishes, textures use it for party decorations, paper flowers, cards, table setting, and notes and more. You can use variety of materials together, materials like, decorative paper, cardstock, foil or fabric to create a unique composition

You can design a wonderful piece on furniture

With cricut explore 3 can with its vinyl add color and texture to a table, your can even use it to design your chair. Use it to cut a photo into a shape

Cricut explorer 3, I am going to tell you how to craft a project with your new machine. We will be doing two crafts with a smart material. So we are going to do a smart vinyl craft and a smart iron on craft. But then I want to also show you how you can put regular materials into your machine by placing them on a mat. So we'll do a project with just regular vinyl through the machine. And then we'll also do a project with regular iron-on with the machine. And those two projects will be on a mat. So one more thing before we get started. When you get your machine this is something that I kind of messed up on and didn't really pay attention to, but when you get your machine your blade is already located and placed into clamp B. But when you get it, make sure you open that clamp and actually make sure that the blade is all the way down. Mine was a little bit up. So when I went to make my first cut, it wasn't cutting through and I started panicking thinking that my machine wasn't cutting. But really, I just had to make sure that the blade was actually all the way down so that it could actually function properly. So make sure you do that just quickly open up clamp B, make sure it's pressed all the way down. You don't have to press it or anything, just make sure that it is down in there. And then you will be all good to go. Okay, so let's go ahead and hop into design space. Okay, so here we are in Cricut Design Space. At this point you have to select the file you are going to be using. I'm going to make a really fun wood sign for the girl's bathroom. I did purchase this from designed bundles. It does come in a bundle with a few other designs in it so you'll have other little designs to choose from as well. So I am going to be using it with the smart vinyl. So what I'm going to do is bring this over here as you can tell, it's made up of multiple different cut layers. So what I want to do is, I want to take everything. That way everything cuts exactly as I see it on the screen. Now what I'm going to do is I'm going to come over to shapes and I'm just going to recreate my circular wooden sign that I will be placing my design on. And my sign is actually white. So I will go ahead and make my circle white. And the size of my sign is actually 13 ½ ". So I will go ahead and size that accordingly. Then I can go ahead and right click and say center front, and bring my design over here that actually in terms of sizing looks pretty good, I might size it up just a little. And I'm going to cut this out have a pink, smart vinyl, so I'll just go ahead and make that pink. Okay, so what I can do now with my circle is I can click on that and just hide it by clicking this eye icon in the Layers panel, I was only using that to actually just size my design, so I don't need that going forward. Okay, so I have my Cricut Explore 3 already selected over here. And now I can say make it. So right here, it wants to know how you are going to load your material into your machine since you do have options. So you can do without a mat, or you can do on a mat or you can do multiple ways. So without and that means that you are using their smart materials. And on a mat, you can use any material to send through the machine. Again,

I'm going to try out the smart vinyl. So I'll go ahead and say without a mat and say done. And then again, we will be doing some other projects with regular vinyl. So I will show you how to load that onto a mat in the project coming up. Okay, so now what I'm going to do is it all looks great. So I can say continue. And then on this screen, I can make my material selection. So I can just say smart vinyl permanent. And then I can load my material into my machine and get this cut out. Okay, so here is the machine, I love the color, I think the color is just perfect, it is what I would have chosen anyway. So I'm really excited with the color that came out. And I also purchased two different colors of the smart vinyl. So I did the pink color, I think this is just called pink. But let me double check. This is actually called light pink. And then I did purchase this champagne color. So that's really pretty as well, of course, I'm sure I will purchase more and more colors. But this is what I purchased to get started. So again, this is the smart vinyl, which means that we can load this without a mat into the machine. So I'll go ahead and open this up and get it loaded. Okay, so I have my smart material here, I will just use the guides that are on the left and right to help guide my material into the machine. And then I'll just push that lightly up against the back little wheels here, then what I can do is I can select this flashing arrow button and it will load my material into the machine. So I went ahead and selected that and it will just automatically pull that into the machine. So there we go. Now what it's going to do is, it's going to measure out my material to make sure I have enough material to complete the cut. And once it's done that, you will see the new play button up here and it is flashing. Now it's flashing because it's already measured and it's ready to go. So then you can go ahead and click that this used to be a little cricket icon. But now it's changed to a little play icon, which means go look how fast that is, oh my goodness, how fun. I can't complain about the speed because I'm really excited that it's a little bit faster. And it'll be really nice to not have to just wait on the machine. Because I find that a lot of the time when I'm crafting, a lot of time is spent kind of twiddling my thumbs waiting for it to cut out so I'm excited that it's a little bit quicker for sure. Actually a lot quicker, it's not a little quicker, it's definitely a lot quicker. Okay, so it's already done. Now I can go ahead again and press the flashing arrows to have it remove the material and we are all ready to go that is so nice. So I can now trim off all of the extra material and get to weeding. Okay, so I'm going to go ahead and start weeding this out. So I just have my little Cricut weeding tool here. And I just like to start in the corner and then just start weeding from there. So I did actually use more pressure on this and it cut perfectly. I love how easy this is to weed out. I personally have always really liked the smart materials, I have found that they are really nice. And it also taught and felt that they are a tad thicker than the regular materials, which I can't complain about. And I actually really like a little bit of a thicker vinyl for glassware. So I know that they did reconfigure the smart vinyl, so I will be curious to see how it or if I notice a difference, but so far, I really, really like it. Okay, so now I'm just going to go through and weed out all of the little centers of the letters. Plus the little bubbles have tiny little centers in there as well that I will really quickly grab and weed out. But I'm really impressed with the weeding, it is working exactly as I thought it would. Okay, so I have a little sample of the Cricut transfer tape that came with my machine here. However, when it comes to the smart material, I've always found that the smart transfer tape, has always worked better for me. So I do like to use their transfer tape when I'm working with the smart material. Again, I noticed that the smart material is a little bit thicker. So I think using their transfer tape that is actually made to work with their product has always, in my opinion, been a better option. So that's just me. But I have found that, that has always been a tried and true way to work with the smart materials. So I'm just placing that on top of my transfer tape so that I can just trim off the amount that I need. And then I will go ahead and get this pulled up off of the final sheet. I like to pierce a little corner just like I would when weeding vinyl, just to get that started. And then I will place that over my design. So I'm going to go ahead and just peel a little bit up at the top here so that I can apply it a little bit easier. So I'm just going to fold that piece down. So I just have a little bit showing there. And I'm going to place that on top of my design and get it lined up. And then I can slowly just peel away the back and then let that transfer take fall onto my design just like this. Okay, there we go. Very easy. And now let's scrape it down. Okay, so I have my little scraper tool, scrape it really well. And then I like to flip mine over and scrape the back down as well. Okay. I just find that scraping the front and back really helps for the next step where you're going to actually take the vinyl off of the cutting sheet and it will come up with the transfer tape. So it's just been a method that's always worked for me. So I like to turn it around. And then I like to just slowly peel away the back, leaving my design on the transfer tape and if there's any pieces that need a little nudging, then I just use my leading tool to help it along. And I honestly think that one of the reasons why it takes a little bit longer to remove the vinyl from this little backer is because it is knotless this backer is so much thicker than a normal backer, so it can be a little bit trickier to maneuver. But as long as you take your time, it is easy. However, if you're used to working with just regular material that's not smart material, the backer is a lot thicker than what you're used to working with. So it can just take a little bit more time because nudging it offers a little bit trickier but it does work fine. Okay, so then we have our design. Let me grab my little sign. This is awesome because at the last minute I am nesting again and I can get even more crafts done that I've been meaning to get done. So I have this cute little wooden base here that I'm going to use. I've had this in my little craft stash for a while now. So I'm going to use this for the little sign for the girl's bathroom. So this is from Hobby Lobby, it looks like 1699. And I'm sure I got it at 40% off, but I'm going to locate where that little hanger is, that way I know where the top is so that it's not hung upside down or my design is placed upside down. So making sure that's right at the top. Okay. And then I can just take my design and place it right on my sign. How cute. So just centering that where I would like it. I think that looks good. Laying it down gently. So sweet. Okay, then what I like to do is take my scraper and start right in the middle, and then just scrape towards the edges. Just like that. I love this color. So cute, it's going to be perfect in their little bathroom. I had that scrape down really well. So I'm just going to grab a little corner here and slowly peel up my transfer tape leaving my design on my sign. And that is peeling off. Okay, so this was the first project I have done with my little Cricut Explore 3, using the smart vinyl permanent, so very impressed, love it. Now let's go ahead and move on to using just regular vinyl with the machine. And then later on, we will use some

Smart Iron-On and then we'll use some regular Iron-On. And we're just going to do a bunch of different little crafts and test a lot of different little products and see how we like how it's going in the machine. Okay, so back in design space really quickly, I am going to go ahead and get my next design all ready to go. Now the purpose of this project is I want to go ahead and place regular material on a mat and send it through my Cricut Explore 3. So for my material, this time, I'm going to use the Oracle 651 permanent vinyl. And we're going to make a little coffee mug. So I'm going to come over to text and I'm going to just personalize my own text and I'm using the font called Mariska. So I have it right here, I have it selected. And then I am going to type out what I would like to say. So I'm just going to say cup show. And I will bring it over into the center here and make this bigger, I will then edit the text. Okay, so now what I'm going to do is come up to alignment, and I'm going to center that. And then I'm going to come to line spacing and decrease the line spacing. And what it will do is it will just decrease that space between the first and second row. And I will just do that until I'm visually happy with how that looks. But what I will do now is just size it for my coffee mug. So I'm thinking about three and a half inches wide. So I will just decrease that to about three and a half. And I might actually go to about three. Okay, that will be just about right. Okay, so now what I'm going to do is I will simply say make it and then it's going to again ask me how I want to place my material through my machine. And this time I'm going to save on and match because again, that's for any material. Okay, so I'll go ahead and select that. This is also an option if you have smart material that is too small to fit through the machine. So if you have already cut down some smart material that you're using as scraps, you can place it on a mat and still use it. Okay, so I can say done. And then you'll see my little design here, I will go ahead and say continue. So now I can go ahead and make my material selection, I can go ahead and browse all materials, browse down to vinyl, and I'll just use the premium outdoor vinyl setting for this. Then I'll go ahead and say done, and then load my material onto my mat. Okay, so again, just opening up my machine and then I'm placing just a little piece of vinyl right onto my mat here. Just had a little scrap that I got from my scrap bin which is perfect for drink-ware. Okay, then I can go ahead and load of my mat into the machine. Again, just following the grids on either side, press the Load button, just like so. Okay, and then I'm going to wait until it has a flashing play button. And then we can get cutting. Right now it says it's measuring the mat length. And after that is done, I can go ahead and say go. Okay, so before doing so I'm going to place that to the side. And what I'm going to do is I'm going to take a little bit of rubbing alcohol, and I'm just going to spray my little glass coffee mug. I purchased this at the Dollar Tree quite a while ago. And I love it. It's just the perfect little shape. And I love a glass coffee mug because my really pretty coffee and creamer just looks so nice in it. Plus, I think the contrast of the really pretty mocha color against the white vinyl is always so pretty, makes a really fun gift.

Okay, so that is drying. Now the rubbing alcohol just helps remove any dust grime or oils. That way your vinyl lays down really nicely. So again, just trimming off all of that extra vinyl, just like that I can use the scraps later. And then I am going to take my weeding tool and I will begin just waiting out my design. And once again, a perfect cut. That's awesome. Okay, so I'll go ahead and grab the little middle pieces really easily and quickly. And then I am going to grab my favorite transfer tape. I really like this this is a clear gridline transfer tape that I really like to use with my regular materials. I'll link it down below but it's one of my favorites to use. So I will go ahead and just trim that down a little bit. And I like a clear transfer tape as well because it makes lining up my project so much easier on the actual base that

I'm placing it on. So placing my transfer tape right over my design, and then again, scraping the top, flipping it over, scraping the back. And then I can go ahead and peel away my carrier sheet. Okay, and then from my coffee mug, I just like to place my little mouse or scraper on either side just to study it while I am getting my vinyl placed on there. And for a circular or more rounded type of base that I'm placing it on like this coffee mug, what I like to do is I like to just trim around my transfer tape. That way it's more flexible when placing it on a curved surface. So being careful of course not to cut into the actual design. But I'm just making that a little bit more flexible so that it takes on the shape of the mug as I'm placing it down, okay. Okay, so here we go, leaving enough room for my lip to sit at the top of the mug. Note that it is not food safe, so you want to avoid the lip area. Okay, and once I have it laid down, then because I have those little cuts in there, I can apply it down in sections. I'll just kind of go from the center and rub towards the edges. Okay. And then I can just go ahead and do the top as well. I like to start with just my fingers and then I go back through with my scraper and really reinforced that. Now of course with vinyl, you will want to make sure that you avoid the dishwasher and avoid the microwave because it is not permanent. And those are super, super fun to make as well. Okay, so just peeling off a transfer tape, making sure there are no bubbles and there's our cute little coffee mug. So easy. Okay, so that was sending through just regular material on a mat through the Cricut Explore 3. Easy to cut out fast and it cuts out really well. And now we can move on to using Smart Iron-On. Okay, so now we are going to use the Cricut Smart Iron-On which again is majlis and we are going to place that through the Cricut Explore 3. So I'm going to use this design to create a little tote bag. I think that will be so cute. I've been wanting to use this design for a while now so I'm really excited to do so. It is made up of multiple layers. So I'm going to go ahead and just weld those all together so that everything cuts exactly where it belongs, you can also attach as well. So now what I'm going to do is simply size my design. So I want this to be eight inches in height. So I'm just going to focus on the height and bring that down to eight. So again, it's asking us how we want to feed our material, because I'm going to be doing Smart Iron-On I will say without a mat and say done, because Iron-

On now I need to mirror my image. So I'm going to toggle the mirror button on and then say continue, I can then go ahead and use the Smart Iron-On setting it's going to remind me to make sure that mirror is turned on which it is I can verify it. And that the Iron-On has material face down, which just means the shiny side is going to be down when feeding it through the machine. Okay, let's go ahead and send this to the machine without a mat. Okay, so now we are ready to go. Now I have my little sample that came in my box. So your sample material might be different, but I had a little bit of smart iron on in mine. So I will go ahead and get this fed through my machine. Now again, you want to locate that shiny side. And that's going to go face down on to the machine here. And then I will go ahead and just line that up on the sides and just push that in till it stops at the little rollers, then I can press the flashing arrows and it will go ahead and auto load my material into the machine. Again, it's going to measure the material to make sure I have enough material to complete the cut. And then I will go ahead and say go and it will go ahead and cut it out. Again, look how fast it goes. That’s really encouraging. Okay, so it's all done, I can go ahead and unload. And that was such a fast cut, I'm really excited. Again, I will go ahead and trim off my smart material and save all of the extra. Again, you can place this on a mat once it is too small to fit knotless through the machine. That way you can still reuse this material but has not been cut. Okay, so with my weeding tool, I will just begin to weed out my design. And I just like to run my weeding tool around and throughout the design just to make sure that my eye tracks every little piece of the design and can check each piece looks great to me. So we'll go ahead and get this on the tote bag over at the heat press and press it on. Okay, so we're back in design space for our final craft. This is the design that I'm going to be using. I did purchase this from design bundles. You could also put this on a tote bag or a coffee mug or some type of drink where there'll be so cute, but I just have to have this on a T shirt. So I'm really excited to use this. So the purpose of this craft is I want to try sending some flock to HTV through my Cricut Explore 3 on a mat. So now I'm going to show you how we can use other regular Iron-On through the Cricut Explore 3 on a map. So what I'm going to simply do is again, it's made up of multiple layers, as you'll see in the Layers panel to your right. So again, I'm just going to weld those altogether. So it is all going to cut out exactly how I see on the screen. And easy all we have to do is size the design. So I'm going to size it at about eight inches, or eight and a half inches across. Let's do about eight and a half. Okay, so that looks good to me. And then I am simply going to say make it so I'm going to cut this out up a white flocked Iron-On and I am going to actually say Automat because this is not smart material. So again, Automat allows you to place any material through the machine. So I will select on a mat say done. Again, since I'm working with Iron-On or HTV those terms are used interchangeably, I can go ahead and mirror my image that's really important because it is Iron-On. So then I can go ahead and say continue. So now I'm going to make my material selection I can say browse all materials. I'm going to say all materials and I'm going to search for flocked and it looks like only flopped paper comes up. So what I'm going to do is I am going to come down to Iron-On and I am going to try to do everyday Iron-On with a more pressure and see if that works. So I will go ahead and say more pressure. Again, I have my mirror turned on and we'll go ahead and get this cut out. Okay, so this is the strip flock pro and this is the flop Iron-On that I am going to be using. I got this from expressions of vinyl. And I've used it before and love it. So I am going to place that shiny side down on to the mat. And then we will place it through with the machine. And then I'm actually going to select my standard grip mat just because this is a much thicker material. So, I want to make sure it stays on the mat really, well. Okay, and this is a brand-new standard grip mat, so this should work just fine. Now of course, always make sure you do a test cut on your machine to make sure you don't waste your material if you're not sure if the cut setting to use for the product that you have. Okay, so we're going to head and load this in. Again, it says it's measuring the mat length. And then once that has been completed, I can go ahead and press the flashing play button which again is our new GO button. Okay, so cutting out really, really well. Okay, so that's all done, I can unload my mats. And again, I will just remove my material and then cut off all of my extra material that has not been cut into. Okay, so now I can just start weeding it. It looks like it cut out perfectly with that cut setting. So I'm super excited about that. Now if you haven't worked with strip flock Pro, it is essentially like a velvet. That's the closest way that I can describe what it actually feels like. So it's really pretty and it makes for a really fun T-shirt and I've done a sweatshirt with it in the wintertime It was really pretty. Okay, so it's a weeding really, really well. Now it does weed a little tough, but the cut is good. So it's just kind of a little bit harder pull off than regular Iron-On but it cuts through flawlessly. Okay, so super simple. Just going through grabbing all those little minute pieces. And then we can get this pressed on to the T-shirt. So the T-shirt that I purchased is Bella and canvas and I'm so impressed with it. I did a Michaels curbside pickup and got it really quickly and it's so soft. I also want to make sure I tell you that I do pre wash my shirts before I put my Iron-On on them. So I did run it through the washer and dryer and it is all ready to go. But then once I turn it over, it is right side up, which is how we will be pressing it on to my shirt. And again, I just run my little weeding tool around my design just to make sure I can see all the pieces and I have everything we did. So let's head to the heat press and get this place on the shirt. Okay, so there we go. Those are the four first crafts that I have done with my Cricut explorer 3, I couldn't be happier and you too can practice this on your own by following the steps I used to achieve mine.

Chapter Five

Troubleshooting

Power button is blinking

Observe when the power button started blinking, then follow the following steps

When powering on your machine: if the power button light is blinking red or is flashing the very first time you turned it on, contact member/customer care for assistance immediately.

When updating firmware: If the power button light is blinking red or it is flashing when you're trying to update your machine's firmware, contact member/customer care for assistance immediately

When loading a smart material or mat: if the power button light is blinking red or is flashing when you're trying to load smart materials or cutting mat, do this;

Check if it occurs with multiple projects; if it is associated to just one project, it could be that an error occurred when saving which resulted to the project being corrupted, the project would have to be recreated. But if it occurs with multiple projects proceed to the step below.

Check if the blade is still sharp: Replace your blade with a new Cricut brand blade. Blades can become dull with use and replacing them with a new, sharp blade often solves this issue.

The roller bar may have gathered some dust or dirt or debris which is resulting in this error. You need to turn the machine off, then carefully and manually move the carriage across the roller bar for four times, this will enable you remove the dirt but if it does not solve the problem contact member/customer care for assistance immediately

In conclusion

The explore 3 has integrated cutting settings. It can print-then-cut on white and colored paper. It has 2x faster cutting speed compared to its predecessors. It also a matless cutting ability when using Smart Materials. Therefore, it is a must have for a faster, cleaner, and better experience in crafting

www.ingramcontent.com/pod-product-compliance
Ingram Content Group UK Ltd.
Pitfield, Milton Keynes, MK11 3LW, UK
UKHW022010190726
13853UKWH00004B/1847

9 798485 071585